50 Delicious Comfort Soup Recipes for Home

By: Kelly Johnson

Table of Contents

- Classic Chicken Noodle Soup
- Creamy Tomato Basil Soup
- Hearty Beef Barley Soup
- Chicken Tortilla Soup
- French Onion Soup
- Creamy Potato Leek Soup
- Spicy Butternut Squash Soup
- Loaded Baked Potato Soup
- Minestrone Soup
- Thai Coconut Chicken Soup
- Creamy Broccoli Cheddar Soup
- New England Clam Chowder
- Vegetable Lentil Soup
- Roasted Red Pepper and Tomato Soup
- Chicken and Wild Rice Soup
- Mushroom Barley Soup
- Moroccan Chickpea Soup
- Tuscan White Bean Soup
- Creamy Corn Chowder
- Beef and Cabbage Soup
- Italian Wedding Soup
- Zucchini Basil Soup
- Pork and Sweet Corn Soup
- Spiced Carrot Soup
- Pea and Ham Soup
- Chicken and Dumplings Soup
- Sweet Potato and Black Bean Soup
- Egg Drop Soup
- Rustic Vegetable Soup
- Greek Lemon Chicken Soup (Avgolemono)
- Roasted Tomato and Garlic Soup
- Spicy Sausage and Kale Soup

- Simple Pho
- Italian Sausage Soup with Kale
- Cheesy Cauliflower Soup
- Creamy Shrimp and Corn Soup
- Beef Stroganoff Soup
- Cabbage Roll Soup
- Sweet and Sour Soup
- Poblano Pepper Soup
- Goulash Soup
- Creamy Celery Soup
- Coconut Curry Soup
- Buffalo Chicken Soup
- Lentil and Spinach Soup
- Wild Mushroom Soup
- Chicken and Orzo Soup
- Spicy Tomato and Chickpea Soup
- Smoky Ham and Bean Soup
- Savory Beef and Ale Soup

Classic Chicken Noodle Soup

Ingredients:

- **For the Soup:**
    - 2 tbsp olive oil
    - 1 large onion, diced
    - 3 cloves garlic, minced
    - 3 large carrots, peeled and sliced
    - 3 celery stalks, sliced
    - 1 tsp dried thyme
    - 1/2 tsp dried rosemary
    - 8 cups chicken broth (or 2 quarts)
    - 2 cups cooked, shredded chicken (preferably from a rotisserie chicken)
    - 2 cups egg noodles (or any pasta of your choice)
    - 1 bay leaf
    - Salt and freshly ground black pepper to taste
    - 1 cup frozen peas (optional)
    - Fresh parsley, chopped (for garnish)

Instructions:

1. **Sauté the Vegetables:**
    - Heat olive oil in a large pot over medium heat.
    - Add the diced onion and cook until softened, about 5 minutes.
    - Stir in the minced garlic and cook for an additional 1 minute.
2. **Add the Carrots and Celery:**
    - Add the sliced carrots and celery to the pot. Cook for about 5 minutes, stirring occasionally.
3. **Add Broth and Seasonings:**
    - Pour in the chicken broth and add the dried thyme, dried rosemary, and bay leaf.
    - Bring to a boil, then reduce heat and let it simmer for 10-15 minutes, or until the vegetables are tender.
4. **Add the Chicken and Noodles:**
    - Stir in the shredded chicken and add the egg noodles.
    - Continue to simmer for about 7-10 minutes, or until the noodles are cooked through.
5. **Finish the Soup:**
    - If using, add the frozen peas and cook for an additional 2-3 minutes.
    - Remove the bay leaf.
    - Season with salt and freshly ground black pepper to taste.
6. **Serve:**

- Ladle the soup into bowls and garnish with freshly chopped parsley if desired.

Tips:

- For extra flavor, you can use homemade chicken broth or add a splash of lemon juice just before serving.
- This soup can be stored in the refrigerator for up to 3 days. It also freezes well; just make sure to cool it completely before freezing.

Enjoy your Classic Chicken Noodle Soup, a comforting bowl of goodness that's perfect for warming up on a chilly day!

Creamy Tomato Basil Soup

Ingredients:

- **2 tbsp olive oil**
- **1 large onion**, chopped
- **3 cloves garlic**, minced
- **2 cans (14.5 oz each) diced tomatoes** (or about 6 cups fresh tomatoes, peeled and chopped)
- **1 cup chicken or vegetable broth**
- **1 cup heavy cream**
- **1/2 cup fresh basil leaves**, chopped (or 2 tbsp dried basil)
- **1 tsp sugar** (optional, to taste)
- **Salt and freshly ground black pepper**, to taste
- **Fresh basil leaves**, for garnish (optional)

Instructions:

1. **Cook the Aromatics:**
   - Heat olive oil in a large pot over medium heat.
   - Add chopped onion and cook until softened, about 5 minutes.
   - Stir in minced garlic and cook for an additional minute until fragrant.
2. **Add Tomatoes and Broth:**
   - Stir in diced tomatoes and their juice. Add chicken or vegetable broth.
   - Bring to a simmer and cook for 15-20 minutes to allow flavors to meld.
3. **Blend the Soup:**
   - Using an immersion blender, blend the soup until smooth. (Alternatively, you can carefully transfer the soup in batches to a blender and blend until smooth.)
4. **Add Cream and Basil:**
   - Return the blended soup to the pot if using a blender. Stir in heavy cream and fresh basil. Add sugar if desired to balance the acidity. Season with salt and pepper to taste.
5. **Heat Through:**
   - Simmer the soup gently for an additional 5 minutes to heat through and allow the flavors to combine.
6. **Serve:**
   - Ladle the soup into bowls. Garnish with fresh basil leaves if desired.

Serve with crusty bread or a grilled cheese sandwich for a comforting meal. Enjoy your creamy and flavorful Tomato Basil Soup!

Hearty Beef Barley Soup

Ingredients:

- **2 tbsp olive oil**
- **1 lb (450 g) beef stew meat**, cut into bite-sized pieces
- **1 large onion**, chopped
- **2 cloves garlic**, minced
- **3 carrots**, sliced
- **2 celery stalks**, sliced
- **1 cup barley**
- **6 cups beef broth**
- **1 cup frozen peas**
- **1 cup chopped tomatoes** (canned or fresh)
- **2 tsp dried thyme**
- **1 tsp dried rosemary**
- **Salt and freshly ground black pepper**, to taste
- **2 tbsp fresh parsley**, chopped (for garnish)

Instructions:

1. **Brown the Beef:**
   - Heat olive oil in a large pot over medium-high heat.
   - Add beef stew meat and cook until browned on all sides. Remove beef from the pot and set aside.
2. **Cook the Vegetables:**
   - In the same pot, add chopped onion, carrots, and celery. Cook until vegetables start to soften, about 5 minutes.
   - Stir in minced garlic and cook for an additional minute.
3. **Add Broth and Barley:**
   - Return the browned beef to the pot.
   - Stir in beef broth, barley, chopped tomatoes, thyme, rosemary, salt, and pepper.
   - Bring to a boil, then reduce heat to low and simmer for about 45 minutes, or until barley and beef are tender.
4. **Add Peas:**
   - Stir in frozen peas and cook for an additional 5 minutes.
5. **Serve:**
   - Ladle the soup into bowls and garnish with fresh parsley.

Enjoy your hearty and comforting Beef Barley Soup!

Chicken Tortilla Soup

Ingredients:

- **2 tbsp olive oil**
- **1 onion**, chopped
- **3 cloves garlic**, minced
- **1 bell pepper**, chopped (red, green, or yellow)
- **2 cups cooked chicken**, shredded (rotisserie chicken works well)
- **1 can (14.5 oz) diced tomatoes**
- **1 can (4 oz) diced green chilies**
- **4 cups chicken broth**
- **1 cup frozen corn**
- **1 tsp ground cumin**
- **1 tsp chili powder**
- **1/2 tsp paprika**
- **1/2 tsp dried oregano**
- **Salt and freshly ground black pepper**, to taste
- **1 cup shredded cheddar cheese** (optional, for topping)
- **1/2 cup fresh cilantro**, chopped (for garnish)
- **Lime wedges**, for serving
- **Tortilla chips**, for serving

Instructions:

1. **Sauté the Aromatics:**
   - Heat olive oil in a large pot over medium heat.
   - Add chopped onion, bell pepper, and garlic. Cook until softened, about 5 minutes.
2. **Add Chicken and Tomatoes:**
   - Stir in shredded chicken, diced tomatoes, and diced green chilies.
3. **Add Broth and Spices:**
   - Pour in chicken broth and add ground cumin, chili powder, paprika, oregano, salt, and pepper.
   - Bring to a boil, then reduce heat and simmer for 20 minutes.
4. **Add Corn:**
   - Stir in frozen corn and cook for an additional 5 minutes.
5. **Serve:**
   - Ladle soup into bowls. Top with shredded cheddar cheese (if using) and garnish with fresh cilantro.
   - Serve with lime wedges and tortilla chips on the side.

Enjoy your flavorful and comforting Chicken Tortilla Soup!

French Onion Soup
Ingredients:

- **4 large onions**, thinly sliced
- **3 tbsp butter**
- **1 tbsp olive oil**
- **2 cloves garlic**, minced
- **1 tsp sugar**
- **1/4 cup dry white wine** (optional)
- **4 cups beef broth** (or a mix of beef and chicken broth)
- **1 bay leaf**
- **1 tsp fresh thyme** (or 1/2 tsp dried thyme)
- **Salt and freshly ground black pepper**, to taste
- **1 baguette**, sliced into 1/2-inch rounds
- **2 cups shredded Gruyère cheese** (or Swiss cheese)
- **1/2 cup grated Parmesan cheese**

Instructions:

1. **Caramelize the Onions:**
    - In a large pot, melt butter with olive oil over medium heat.
    - Add onions and cook, stirring frequently, until they are deeply browned and caramelized, about 30-40 minutes.
    - Stir in minced garlic and sugar, cooking for an additional 2 minutes.
2. **Deglaze and Simmer:**
    - If using, pour in white wine and cook for 2-3 minutes, scraping up any browned bits from the bottom of the pot.
    - Add beef broth, bay leaf, and thyme. Bring to a simmer and cook for 20 minutes. Season with salt and pepper to taste.
3. **Prepare the Bread:**
    - While the soup is simmering, preheat the broiler. Arrange baguette slices on a baking sheet and toast under the broiler until golden brown on both sides.
4. **Assemble and Broil:**
    - Ladle the soup into oven-safe bowls. Place a toasted baguette slice on top of each bowl and sprinkle with Gruyère and Parmesan cheese.
    - Place the bowls under the broiler until the cheese is melted and bubbly, about 2-3 minutes. Watch closely to avoid burning.
5. **Serve:**
    - Carefully remove the hot bowls from the oven. Serve the soup immediately.

Enjoy your rich and comforting French Onion Soup!

Creamy Potato Leek Soup

Ingredients:

- **2 tbsp olive oil**
- **2 leeks**, cleaned and sliced (white and light green parts only)
- **3 cloves garlic**, minced
- **4 cups potatoes**, peeled and diced (about 4 medium potatoes)
- **4 cups chicken or vegetable broth**
- **1 cup heavy cream** (or milk for a lighter version)
- **1 tsp dried thyme** (or 2 tsp fresh thyme)
- **Salt and freshly ground black pepper**, to taste
- **2 tbsp fresh chives**, chopped (for garnish, optional)

Instructions:

1. **Sauté the Leeks and Garlic:**
   - Heat olive oil in a large pot over medium heat.
   - Add sliced leeks and cook until softened, about 5 minutes.
   - Stir in minced garlic and cook for an additional 1 minute until fragrant.
2. **Add Potatoes and Broth:**
   - Add diced potatoes and cook for 2-3 minutes, stirring occasionally.
   - Pour in chicken or vegetable broth and add dried thyme.
   - Bring to a boil, then reduce heat and simmer for 20 minutes, or until potatoes are tender.
3. **Blend the Soup:**
   - Using an immersion blender, blend the soup until smooth and creamy. (Alternatively, you can carefully transfer the soup in batches to a blender and blend until smooth.)
4. **Add Cream and Season:**
   - Return the blended soup to the pot if using a blender. Stir in heavy cream and heat through.
   - Season with salt and freshly ground black pepper to taste.
5. **Serve:**
   - Ladle the soup into bowls. Garnish with fresh chives if desired.

Enjoy your creamy and comforting Potato Leek Soup!

Spicy Butternut Squash Soup

Ingredients:

- **2 tbsp olive oil**
- **1 large onion**, chopped
- **2 cloves garlic**, minced
- **1 tbsp fresh ginger**, minced
- **1 medium butternut squash**, peeled, seeded, and cubed
- **1 carrot**, peeled and chopped
- **4 cups vegetable or chicken broth**
- **1 can (14.5 oz) coconut milk**
- **1-2 tsp ground cumin**
- **1/2-1 tsp cayenne pepper** (adjust to taste)
- **1/2 tsp smoked paprika**
- **Salt and freshly ground black pepper**, to taste
- **2 tbsp fresh cilantro**, chopped (for garnish)

Instructions:

1. **Sauté the Aromatics:**
    - Heat olive oil in a large pot over medium heat.
    - Add chopped onion and cook until softened, about 5 minutes.
    - Stir in minced garlic and ginger, cooking for another minute.
2. **Add Vegetables:**
    - Add butternut squash and carrot to the pot. Cook for 5 minutes, stirring occasionally.
3. **Add Broth and Spices:**
    - Pour in vegetable or chicken broth. Stir in ground cumin, cayenne pepper, smoked paprika, salt, and pepper.
    - Bring to a boil, then reduce heat and simmer for 20-25 minutes, or until squash and carrot are tender.
4. **Blend the Soup:**
    - Using an immersion blender, blend the soup until smooth and creamy. (Alternatively, carefully transfer the soup in batches to a blender and blend until smooth.)
5. **Add Coconut Milk:**
    - Stir in the coconut milk and heat through. Adjust seasoning if needed.
6. **Serve:**
    - Ladle soup into bowls and garnish with fresh cilantro.

Enjoy your spicy and creamy Butternut Squash Soup!

Loaded Baked Potato Soup

Ingredients:

- **4 large russet potatoes**, peeled and diced
- **4 slices bacon**, chopped
- **1 medium onion**, chopped
- **3 cloves garlic**, minced
- **1/4 cup all-purpose flour**
- **4 cups chicken or vegetable broth**
- **1 cup milk** (whole or 2%)
- **1 cup shredded cheddar cheese**
- **1/2 cup sour cream**
- **Salt and freshly ground black pepper**, to taste
- **2 green onions**, sliced (for garnish)
- **Extra shredded cheddar cheese**, for topping
- **Additional crumbled bacon**, for topping (optional)

Instructions:

1. **Cook the Bacon:**
   - In a large pot, cook chopped bacon over medium heat until crispy. Remove bacon and drain on paper towels. Discard excess bacon fat, leaving about 1 tablespoon in the pot.
2. **Sauté Onions and Garlic:**
   - Add chopped onion to the pot and cook until softened, about 5 minutes.
   - Stir in minced garlic and cook for an additional minute.
3. **Cook the Potatoes:**
   - Add diced potatoes and cook for 5 minutes, stirring occasionally.
4. **Make the Soup Base:**
   - Sprinkle flour over the potatoes and onions. Stir to coat and cook for 2 minutes.
   - Gradually add chicken or vegetable broth, stirring constantly. Bring to a boil, then reduce heat and simmer until potatoes are tender, about 15 minutes.
5. **Blend (Optional):**
   - For a smoother texture, use an immersion blender to blend some of the soup. Alternatively, mash the potatoes with a potato masher.
6. **Add Cream and Cheese:**
   - Stir in milk, shredded cheddar cheese, and sour cream. Cook until the cheese is melted and the soup is heated through. Season with salt and pepper to taste.
7. **Serve:**
   - Ladle the soup into bowls. Top with additional shredded cheddar cheese, crumbled bacon, and sliced green onions.

Enjoy your hearty and comforting Loaded Baked Potato Soup!

Minestrone Soup

Ingredients:

- **2 tbsp olive oil**
- **1 large onion**, chopped
- **2 cloves garlic**, minced
- **2 carrots**, peeled and diced
- **2 celery stalks**, diced
- **1 medium zucchini**, diced
- **1 cup green beans**, trimmed and cut into bite-sized pieces
- **1 cup potatoes**, peeled and diced
- **1 cup canned diced tomatoes** (or fresh, peeled and chopped)
- **4 cups vegetable or chicken broth**
- **1 can (15 oz) kidney beans**, drained and rinsed
- **1 cup cooked pasta** (e.g., ditalini or elbow macaroni)
- **1 cup frozen peas**
- **1 tsp dried basil**
- **1 tsp dried oregano**
- **1/2 tsp dried thyme**
- **Salt and freshly ground black pepper**, to taste
- **1/4 cup fresh parsley**, chopped (for garnish)
- **Grated Parmesan cheese**, for serving (optional)

Instructions:

1. **Sauté the Vegetables:**
   - Heat olive oil in a large pot over medium heat.
   - Add chopped onion, carrots, and celery. Cook until vegetables are softened, about 5-7 minutes.
   - Stir in minced garlic and cook for an additional 1 minute.
2. **Add Remaining Vegetables:**
   - Add zucchini, green beans, and potatoes to the pot. Cook for 5 minutes, stirring occasionally.
3. **Add Tomatoes and Broth:**
   - Stir in diced tomatoes and pour in vegetable or chicken broth.
   - Bring to a boil, then reduce heat and simmer until the vegetables are tender, about 20 minutes.
4. **Add Beans and Pasta:**
   - Stir in kidney beans, cooked pasta, and frozen peas. Simmer for an additional 5-10 minutes to heat through.
5. **Season and Garnish:**
   - Add dried basil, oregano, thyme, salt, and pepper. Stir to combine.
   - Garnish with fresh parsley before serving.
6. **Serve:**
   - Ladle soup into bowls and sprinkle with grated Parmesan cheese if desired.

Enjoy your comforting and nutritious Minestrone Soup!

Thai Coconut Chicken Soup

Ingredients:

- **1 tbsp vegetable oil**
- **1 lb (450 g) chicken breasts or thighs**, thinly sliced
- **1 onion**, chopped
- **3 cloves garlic**, minced
- **1 tbsp fresh ginger**, minced
- **1-2 tbsp red curry paste** (adjust to taste)
- **1 can (14 oz) coconut milk**
- **3 cups chicken broth**
- **1 cup sliced mushrooms** (e.g., shiitake or button)
- **1 red bell pepper**, sliced
- **1 cup baby spinach** or **kale**
- **2 tbsp fish sauce** (or soy sauce for a vegetarian option)
- **1-2 tbsp lime juice** (to taste)
- **1 tbsp brown sugar**
- **Fresh cilantro**, chopped (for garnish)
- **Lime wedges**, for serving
- **Cooked rice** or **rice noodles**, for serving

Instructions:

1. **Cook the Chicken:**
   - Heat vegetable oil in a large pot over medium heat.
   - Add sliced chicken and cook until no longer pink. Remove chicken from the pot and set aside.
2. **Sauté Aromatics:**
   - In the same pot, add onion and cook until softened, about 5 minutes.
   - Stir in garlic, ginger, and red curry paste, cooking for 1-2 minutes until fragrant.
3. **Add Liquids and Vegetables:**
   - Pour in coconut milk and chicken broth, stirring to combine.
   - Add mushrooms and red bell pepper. Bring to a simmer and cook for about 10 minutes until vegetables are tender.
4. **Finish the Soup:**
   - Return the cooked chicken to the pot. Stir in baby spinach or kale, fish sauce, lime juice, and brown sugar.
   - Simmer for an additional 2-3 minutes until the greens are wilted and the soup is heated through.
5. **Serve:**
   - Ladle soup into bowls. Garnish with fresh cilantro and serve with lime wedges.
   - Add cooked rice or rice noodles to the bowls if desired.

Enjoy your aromatic and comforting Thai Coconut Chicken Soup!

Creamy Broccoli Cheddar Soup

Ingredients:

- **2 tbsp butter**
- **1 large onion**, chopped
- **3 cloves garlic**, minced
- **4 cups broccoli florets** (about 1 medium head of broccoli)
- **2 cups vegetable or chicken broth**
- **1 cup milk** (whole or 2%)
- **1 cup heavy cream**
- **2 cups shredded cheddar cheese** (sharp or mild, based on preference)
- **1/4 cup all-purpose flour**
- **1/2 tsp dried thyme** (or 1 tsp fresh thyme)
- **Salt and freshly ground black pepper**, to taste
- **Optional: 1/2 cup grated Parmesan cheese** (for extra richness)

Instructions:

1. **Sauté the Aromatics:**
    - In a large pot, melt butter over medium heat.
    - Add chopped onion and cook until softened, about 5 minutes.
    - Stir in minced garlic and cook for an additional 1 minute.
2. **Cook the Broccoli:**
    - Add broccoli florets to the pot and cook for about 5 minutes.
    - Sprinkle flour over the broccoli and stir well to coat. Cook for 1-2 minutes to eliminate the raw flour taste.
3. **Add Broth and Simmer:**
    - Gradually pour in vegetable or chicken broth, stirring constantly.
    - Bring to a boil, then reduce heat and simmer until broccoli is tender, about 10-15 minutes.
4. **Blend the Soup:**
    - Use an immersion blender to blend the soup until smooth. (Alternatively, carefully transfer the soup in batches to a blender and blend until smooth.)
5. **Add Cream and Cheese:**
    - Return the blended soup to the pot if using a blender. Stir in milk and heavy cream.
    - Heat the soup gently over medium heat (do not boil). Gradually add shredded cheddar cheese and stir until melted and smooth.
    - If using, stir in grated Parmesan cheese for extra richness.
6. **Season and Serve:**
    - Season with dried thyme, salt, and freshly ground black pepper to taste.
    - Serve hot, optionally garnished with extra cheddar cheese or a sprinkle of fresh herbs.

Enjoy your creamy and cheesy Broccoli Cheddar Soup!

New England Clam Chowder

Ingredients:

- **4 slices bacon**, chopped
- **1 large onion**, chopped
- **2 cloves garlic**, minced
- **3 celery stalks**, chopped
- **1 large potato**, peeled and diced
- **1/4 cup all-purpose flour**
- **2 cups chicken or clam broth**
- **1 cup heavy cream**
- **1 cup milk** (whole or 2%)
- **2 cans (6.5 oz each) chopped clams**, with juice
- **1 bay leaf**
- **1/2 tsp dried thyme**
- **Salt and freshly ground black pepper**, to taste
- **2 tbsp fresh parsley**, chopped (for garnish)

Instructions:

1. **Cook the Bacon:**
   - In a large pot, cook chopped bacon over medium heat until crispy. Remove bacon and drain on paper towels. Discard excess bacon fat, leaving about 1 tablespoon in the pot.
2. **Sauté Vegetables:**
   - Add chopped onion, celery, and garlic to the pot. Cook until softened, about 5 minutes.
3. **Add Potatoes and Flour:**
   - Stir in diced potatoes and cook for 2 minutes.
   - Sprinkle flour over the vegetables and stir well. Cook for 1-2 minutes to eliminate the raw flour taste.
4. **Add Broth and Simmer:**
   - Gradually pour in chicken or clam broth, stirring constantly. Add bay leaf and dried thyme.
   - Bring to a boil, then reduce heat and simmer until potatoes are tender, about 15 minutes.
5. **Add Clams and Cream:**
   - Stir in heavy cream, milk, and chopped clams with their juice. Heat gently, being careful not to boil.
6. **Season and Serve:**
   - Remove bay leaf. Season with salt and pepper to taste.
   - Serve hot, garnished with crispy bacon and fresh parsley.

Enjoy your rich and creamy New England Clam Chowder!

Vegetable Lentil Soup

Ingredients:

- **2 tbsp olive oil**
- **1 large onion**, chopped
- **3 cloves garlic**, minced
- **2 carrots**, peeled and diced
- **2 celery stalks**, diced
- **1 bell pepper**, chopped (any color)
- **1 cup dried green or brown lentils**, rinsed and drained
- **1 can (14.5 oz) diced tomatoes** (or 2 cups fresh tomatoes, peeled and chopped)
- **6 cups vegetable broth** (or chicken broth)
- **1 cup chopped kale** or **spinach** (optional)
- **1 tsp ground cumin**
- **1/2 tsp smoked paprika**
- **1/2 tsp dried thyme** (or 1 tsp fresh thyme)
- **1 bay leaf**
- **Salt and freshly ground black pepper**, to taste
- **1 cup frozen peas** (optional, for extra color and nutrition)
- **2 tbsp fresh parsley**, chopped (for garnish)

Instructions:

1. **Sauté Vegetables:**
   - Heat olive oil in a large pot over medium heat.
   - Add chopped onion, carrots, celery, and bell pepper. Cook until vegetables are softened, about 5-7 minutes.
   - Stir in minced garlic and cook for an additional minute.
2. **Add Lentils and Spices:**
   - Stir in rinsed lentils, ground cumin, smoked paprika, dried thyme, and bay leaf. Cook for 2 minutes.
3. **Add Tomatoes and Broth:**
   - Add diced tomatoes and pour in vegetable broth.
   - Bring to a boil, then reduce heat and simmer for about 30-35 minutes, or until lentils and vegetables are tender.
4. **Add Greens and Peas:**
   - Stir in chopped kale or spinach (if using) and frozen peas. Simmer for an additional 5 minutes.
5. **Season and Serve:**
   - Remove the bay leaf. Season with salt and freshly ground black pepper to taste.
   - Garnish with fresh parsley before serving.

Enjoy your nourishing and flavorful Vegetable Lentil Soup!

Roasted Red Pepper and Tomato Soup

Ingredients:

- **4 large red bell peppers**, halved and seeded

- **1 tbsp olive oil**
- **1 large onion**, chopped
- **3 cloves garlic**, minced
- **1 can (14.5 oz) diced tomatoes**
- **1 cup vegetable or chicken broth**
- **1 cup heavy cream** (or milk for a lighter version)
- **1 tsp dried basil** (or 2 tsp fresh basil)
- **1/2 tsp dried thyme** (or 1 tsp fresh thyme)
- **Salt and freshly ground black pepper**, to taste
- **1 tbsp balsamic vinegar** (optional, for added depth)
- **Fresh basil leaves**, for garnish (optional)

Instructions:

1. **Roast the Red Peppers:**
   - Preheat your oven to 425°F (220°C).
   - Place red bell pepper halves on a baking sheet, skin side up. Drizzle with olive oil.
   - Roast in the oven for 20-25 minutes, or until the skins are blackened and blistered.
   - Remove from oven and place peppers in a bowl. Cover with plastic wrap and let them steam for 10 minutes. Peel off the skins once cooled.
2. **Sauté Aromatics:**
   - While the peppers are roasting, heat olive oil in a large pot over medium heat.
   - Add chopped onion and cook until softened, about 5 minutes.
   - Stir in minced garlic and cook for an additional minute.
3. **Combine Ingredients:**
   - Add peeled, roasted red peppers, diced tomatoes (with their juice), and vegetable or chicken broth to the pot.
   - Bring to a boil, then reduce heat and simmer for 10-15 minutes to allow flavors to meld.
4. **Blend the Soup:**
   - Use an immersion blender to blend the soup until smooth and creamy. (Alternatively, carefully transfer the soup in batches to a blender and blend until smooth.)
5. **Add Cream and Seasonings:**
   - Stir in heavy cream and heat through.
   - Season with dried basil, thyme, salt, and freshly ground black pepper to taste.
   - Add balsamic vinegar if desired for extra depth of flavor.
6. **Serve:**
   - Ladle the soup into bowls and garnish with fresh basil leaves if desired.

Enjoy your rich and flavorful Roasted Red Pepper and Tomato Soup!

Chicken and Wild Rice Soup

Ingredients:

- 2 tbsp olive oil

- **1 large onion**, chopped
- **2 cloves garlic**, minced
- **2 celery stalks**, diced
- **2 carrots**, peeled and diced
- **1 cup wild rice**, rinsed
- **4 cups chicken broth**
- **1 cup cooked chicken**, shredded or diced (use rotisserie or leftover chicken)
- **1 cup frozen peas**
- **1 cup heavy cream** (or milk for a lighter version)
- **1 tsp dried thyme** (or 2 tsp fresh thyme)
- **1/2 tsp dried rosemary**
- **Salt and freshly ground black pepper**, to taste
- **2 tbsp fresh parsley**, chopped (for garnish)

Instructions:

1. **Sauté the Vegetables:**
    - Heat olive oil in a large pot over medium heat.
    - Add chopped onion, celery, and carrots. Cook until softened, about 5-7 minutes.
    - Stir in minced garlic and cook for an additional minute.
2. **Cook the Rice:**
    - Add rinsed wild rice to the pot. Cook for 2 minutes, stirring occasionally.
3. **Add Broth and Simmer:**
    - Pour in chicken broth and bring to a boil.
    - Reduce heat and simmer for 40-45 minutes, or until wild rice is tender.
4. **Add Chicken and Peas:**
    - Stir in cooked chicken and frozen peas. Simmer for 5 minutes.
5. **Add Cream and Seasonings:**
    - Stir in heavy cream and cook until heated through.
    - Add dried thyme, rosemary, salt, and freshly ground black pepper to taste.
6. **Serve:**
    - Ladle soup into bowls and garnish with fresh parsley.

Enjoy your hearty and creamy Chicken and Wild Rice Soup!

Mushroom Barley Soup

Ingredients:

- 2 tbsp olive oil

- **1 large onion**, chopped
- **3 cloves garlic**, minced
- **2 cups mushrooms**, sliced (such as cremini or button mushrooms)
- **2 carrots**, peeled and diced
- **2 celery stalks**, diced
- **1 cup pearl barley**, rinsed
- **4 cups vegetable or beef broth**
- **1 cup water** (or additional broth)
- **1 tsp dried thyme** (or 2 tsp fresh thyme)
- **1 bay leaf**
- **Salt and freshly ground black pepper**, to taste
- **2 tbsp soy sauce** (optional, for depth of flavor)
- **1/2 cup fresh parsley**, chopped (for garnish)

Instructions:

1. **Sauté the Vegetables:**
    - Heat olive oil in a large pot over medium heat.
    - Add chopped onion and cook until softened, about 5 minutes.
    - Stir in minced garlic and cook for another minute.
2. **Cook the Mushrooms:**
    - Add sliced mushrooms to the pot. Cook until mushrooms release their moisture and begin to brown, about 5-7 minutes.
3. **Add Carrots and Celery:**
    - Stir in diced carrots and celery. Cook for another 5 minutes.
4. **Add Barley and Broth:**
    - Add rinsed pearl barley, vegetable or beef broth, and water to the pot. Stir to combine.
    - Add dried thyme, bay leaf, and soy sauce if using.
5. **Simmer:**
    - Bring the soup to a boil, then reduce heat and let it simmer for 30-40 minutes, or until barley is tender and the vegetables are cooked through.
6. **Season and Serve:**
    - Remove the bay leaf. Season with salt and freshly ground black pepper to taste.
    - Garnish with fresh parsley before serving.

Enjoy your hearty and flavorful Mushroom Barley Soup!

Moroccan Chickpea Soup

Ingredients:

- **2 tbsp olive oil**

- **1 large onion**, chopped
- **3 cloves garlic**, minced
- **1 tbsp fresh ginger**, minced
- **1 large carrot**, peeled and diced
- **1 red bell pepper**, diced
- **2 tsp ground cumin**
- **1 tsp ground coriander**
- **1/2 tsp ground cinnamon**
- **1/4 tsp ground turmeric**
- **1/4 tsp cayenne pepper** (optional, for heat)
- **1 can (14.5 oz) diced tomatoes**
- **2 cans (15 oz each) chickpeas**, drained and rinsed
- **4 cups vegetable or chicken broth**
- **1 cup cooked quinoa** or **couscous** (optional, for added texture)
- **1 cup baby spinach** or **kale** (optional)
- **1 tbsp lemon juice**
- **Salt and freshly ground black pepper**, to taste
- **2 tbsp fresh cilantro**, chopped (for garnish)
- **2 tbsp fresh parsley**, chopped (for garnish)

Instructions:

1. **Sauté Aromatics:**
   - Heat olive oil in a large pot over medium heat.
   - Add chopped onion and cook until softened, about 5 minutes.
   - Stir in minced garlic and ginger, and cook for another minute.
2. **Add Vegetables and Spices:**
   - Add diced carrot and red bell pepper to the pot. Cook for 5 minutes.
   - Stir in ground cumin, coriander, cinnamon, turmeric, and cayenne pepper if using. Cook for 1-2 minutes until fragrant.
3. **Add Tomatoes and Chickpeas:**
   - Stir in diced tomatoes and cook for a few minutes.
   - Add chickpeas and pour in vegetable or chicken broth. Bring to a boil.
4. **Simmer:**
   - Reduce heat and let the soup simmer for 20-25 minutes, or until vegetables are tender.
5. **Add Greens and Quinoa/Couscous:**
   - Stir in cooked quinoa or couscous and baby spinach or kale if using. Simmer for an additional 5 minutes.
6. **Season and Serve:**
   - Add lemon juice and season with salt and freshly ground black pepper to taste.
   - Garnish with fresh cilantro and parsley before serving.

Enjoy your aromatic and hearty Moroccan Chickpea Soup!

Tuscan White Bean Soup

Ingredients:

- **2 tbsp olive oil**
- **1 large onion**, chopped

- **2 cloves garlic**, minced
- **2 carrots**, peeled and diced
- **2 celery stalks**, diced
- **1 tsp dried rosemary** (or 1 tbsp fresh rosemary, chopped)
- **1 tsp dried thyme** (or 1 tbsp fresh thyme, chopped)
- **1/2 tsp dried sage** (optional)
- **1 can (14.5 oz) diced tomatoes**
- **2 cans (15 oz each) white beans** (such as cannellini or great northern), drained and rinsed
- **4 cups vegetable or chicken broth**
- **1 cup baby spinach** or **kale** (optional)
- **1 cup cooked pasta** (e.g., ditalini or small shells, optional)
- **Salt and freshly ground black pepper**, to taste
- **1 tbsp balsamic vinegar** (optional, for added depth)
- **2 tbsp fresh parsley**, chopped (for garnish)
- **Grated Parmesan cheese**, for serving (optional)

Instructions:

1. **Sauté Vegetables:**
    - Heat olive oil in a large pot over medium heat.
    - Add chopped onion, carrots, and celery. Cook until vegetables are softened, about 5-7 minutes.
    - Stir in minced garlic and cook for another minute.
2. **Add Herbs and Tomatoes:**
    - Stir in dried rosemary, thyme, and sage if using. Cook for 1-2 minutes until fragrant.
    - Add diced tomatoes and cook for a few minutes.
3. **Add Beans and Broth:**
    - Stir in white beans and pour in vegetable or chicken broth. Bring to a boil.
    - Reduce heat and let the soup simmer for 20-25 minutes to allow flavors to meld.
4. **Add Greens and Pasta:**
    - Stir in baby spinach or kale and cooked pasta if using. Simmer for an additional 5 minutes until the greens are wilted and the pasta is heated through.
5. **Season and Serve:**
    - Season with salt and freshly ground black pepper to taste.
    - Add balsamic vinegar if desired for extra depth.
    - Garnish with fresh parsley and serve with grated Parmesan cheese if desired.

Enjoy your hearty and flavorful Tuscan White Bean Soup!

Creamy Corn Chowder

Ingredients:

- **2 tbsp butter**
- **1 large onion**, chopped

- **2 cloves garlic**, minced
- **2 celery stalks**, diced
- **1 red bell pepper**, diced
- **4 cups fresh or frozen corn kernels** (about 4-5 ears of corn or 2 cups frozen)
- **1 large potato**, peeled and diced
- **4 cups chicken or vegetable broth**
- **1 cup heavy cream** (or milk for a lighter version)
- **1 cup whole milk**
- **1 tsp dried thyme** (or 2 tsp fresh thyme)
- **1/2 tsp smoked paprika** (optional)
- **Salt and freshly ground black pepper**, to taste
- **2 tbsp all-purpose flour** (for thickening, optional)
- **2 tbsp fresh parsley**, chopped (for garnish)
- **Optional: Crumbled bacon or shredded cheddar cheese**, for topping

Instructions:

1. **Sauté the Vegetables:**
    - In a large pot, melt butter over medium heat.
    - Add chopped onion, celery, and red bell pepper. Cook until vegetables are softened, about 5 minutes.
    - Stir in minced garlic and cook for an additional minute.
2. **Add Corn and Potato:**
    - Stir in corn kernels and diced potato. Cook for 2-3 minutes.
3. **Add Broth and Simmer:**
    - Pour in chicken or vegetable broth and bring to a boil.
    - Reduce heat and simmer until potatoes are tender, about 15-20 minutes.
4. **Blend (Optional):**
    - For a smoother texture, use an immersion blender to partially or fully blend the soup. Alternatively, carefully transfer a portion of the soup to a blender, blend until smooth, and return it to the pot.
5. **Add Cream and Seasonings:**
    - Stir in heavy cream and whole milk. Heat gently (do not boil).
    - Add dried thyme, smoked paprika if using, salt, and freshly ground black pepper to taste.
    - If you prefer a thicker chowder, mix 2 tablespoons of flour with a small amount of water to create a slurry and stir it into the soup. Simmer for a few additional minutes until thickened.
6. **Serve:**
    - Ladle soup into bowls and garnish with fresh parsley. Optionally, top with crumbled bacon or shredded cheddar cheese.

Enjoy your rich and creamy Corn Chowder!

Beef and Cabbage Soup

Ingredients:

- **2 tbsp olive oil**
- **1 lb (450 g) beef stew meat**, cut into cubes
- **1 large onion**, chopped
- **3 cloves garlic**, minced

- **2 carrots**, peeled and diced
- **2 celery stalks**, diced
- **1 small head of cabbage**, chopped (about 4 cups)
- **1 can (14.5 oz) diced tomatoes**
- **4 cups beef broth**
- **2 cups water** (or additional beef broth)
- **1 tsp dried thyme** (or 2 tsp fresh thyme)
- **1 bay leaf**
- **1/2 tsp paprika**
- **Salt and freshly ground black pepper**, to taste
- **1 cup frozen peas** (optional)
- **2 tbsp fresh parsley**, chopped (for garnish)

Instructions:

1. **Brown the Beef:**
    - Heat olive oil in a large pot over medium-high heat.
    - Add beef cubes and cook until browned on all sides. Remove beef from the pot and set aside.
2. **Sauté Vegetables:**
    - In the same pot, add chopped onion, carrots, and celery. Cook until vegetables are softened, about 5-7 minutes.
    - Stir in minced garlic and cook for an additional minute.
3. **Add Cabbage and Beef:**
    - Add chopped cabbage to the pot and cook for 5 minutes, stirring occasionally.
    - Return browned beef to the pot.
4. **Add Broth and Simmer:**
    - Stir in diced tomatoes, beef broth, and water.
    - Add dried thyme, bay leaf, paprika, salt, and freshly ground black pepper.
    - Bring to a boil, then reduce heat and simmer for 30-40 minutes, or until beef is tender.
5. **Add Peas (Optional):**
    - Stir in frozen peas and cook for an additional 5 minutes.
6. **Serve:**
    - Remove bay leaf. Adjust seasoning with salt and pepper if needed.
    - Garnish with fresh parsley before serving.

Enjoy your hearty and satisfying Beef and Cabbage Soup!

Italian Wedding Soup

Ingredients:

- **For the Meatballs:**
    - 1/2 lb (225 g) ground beef
    - 1/2 lb (225 g) ground pork
    - 1/4 cup grated Parmesan cheese

- 1/4 cup fresh parsley, chopped
- 1/4 cup bread crumbs
- 1 egg
- 2 cloves garlic, minced
- Salt and freshly ground black pepper, to taste
- **For the Soup:**
  - 1 tbsp olive oil
  - 1 large onion, chopped
  - 2 cloves garlic, minced
  - 2 carrots, peeled and diced
  - 2 celery stalks, diced
  - 8 cups chicken broth
  - 1 cup small pasta (such as acini di pepe or orzo)
  - 2 cups fresh spinach or kale, chopped
  - 1 tsp dried thyme (or 2 tsp fresh thyme)
  - Salt and freshly ground black pepper, to taste
  - 2 tbsp fresh parsley, chopped (for garnish)
  - Grated Parmesan cheese, for serving

Instructions:

1. **Make the Meatballs:**
   - In a bowl, combine ground beef, ground pork, grated Parmesan cheese, fresh parsley, bread crumbs, egg, minced garlic, salt, and pepper.
   - Mix until well combined. Form into small meatballs, about 1 inch in diameter.
2. **Cook the Meatballs:**
   - Heat a large pot over medium heat. Add a little olive oil if needed.
   - Brown meatballs in batches until cooked through. Remove from the pot and set aside.
3. **Sauté Vegetables:**
   - In the same pot, add olive oil if needed. Sauté chopped onion, carrots, and celery until softened, about 5-7 minutes.
   - Stir in minced garlic and cook for an additional minute.
4. **Add Broth and Pasta:**
   - Pour in chicken broth and bring to a boil.
   - Add small pasta and cook according to package instructions, until al dente.
5. **Add Meatballs and Greens:**
   - Return meatballs to the pot. Stir in fresh spinach or kale.
   - Simmer until greens are wilted and meatballs are heated through.
6. **Season and Serve:**
   - Season with dried thyme, salt, and freshly ground black pepper to taste.
   - Garnish with fresh parsley and serve with grated Parmesan cheese.

Enjoy your comforting Italian Wedding Soup!

Zucchini Basil Soup

Ingredients:

- **2 tbsp olive oil**
- **1 large onion**, chopped
- **3 cloves garlic**, minced
- **4 cups zucchini**, diced (about 4 medium zucchinis)

- **4 cups vegetable or chicken broth**
- **1 cup fresh basil leaves**, packed
- **1/2 cup heavy cream** (or milk for a lighter version)
- **Salt and freshly ground black pepper**, to taste
- **1/2 tsp dried thyme** (optional)
- **2 tbsp fresh basil**, chopped (for garnish)

Instructions:

1. **Sauté Vegetables:**
   - Heat olive oil in a large pot over medium heat.
   - Add chopped onion and cook until softened, about 5 minutes.
   - Stir in minced garlic and cook for an additional minute.
2. **Add Zucchini:**
   - Add diced zucchini to the pot. Cook for 5-7 minutes, stirring occasionally, until zucchini is softened.
3. **Add Broth and Simmer:**
   - Pour in vegetable or chicken broth. Bring to a boil.
   - Reduce heat and simmer for 15-20 minutes, until zucchini is very tender.
4. **Blend the Soup:**
   - Use an immersion blender to blend the soup until smooth. Alternatively, carefully transfer soup in batches to a blender, blend until smooth, and return to the pot.
5. **Add Cream and Basil:**
   - Stir in heavy cream and cook gently until heated through.
   - Add fresh basil leaves and blend again until basil is finely incorporated into the soup. (Alternatively, you can chop basil and stir it in after blending.)
6. **Season and Serve:**
   - Season with salt, freshly ground black pepper, and dried thyme if using.
   - Garnish with fresh chopped basil before serving.

Enjoy your vibrant and creamy Zucchini Basil Soup!

Pork and Sweet Corn Soup

Ingredients:

- **2 tbsp vegetable oil**
- **1 lb (450 g) pork tenderloin**, thinly sliced or cubed
- **1 large onion**, chopped
- **3 cloves garlic**, minced

- **2 carrots**, peeled and sliced
- **2 celery stalks**, diced
- **4 cups chicken or vegetable broth**
- **2 cups fresh or frozen sweet corn kernels**
- **1 cup mushrooms**, sliced (optional)
- **1 tsp ground ginger** (or 1 tbsp fresh ginger, minced)
- **1/2 tsp soy sauce** (optional, for added depth)
- **Salt and freshly ground black pepper**, to taste
- **2 tbsp fresh cilantro** or **parsley**, chopped (for garnish)

Instructions:

1. **Cook the Pork:**
   - Heat vegetable oil in a large pot over medium-high heat.
   - Add pork and cook until browned and cooked through, about 4-5 minutes. Remove pork from the pot and set aside.
2. **Sauté Vegetables:**
   - In the same pot, add chopped onion, carrots, and celery. Cook until vegetables are softened, about 5-7 minutes.
   - Stir in minced garlic and cook for an additional minute.
3. **Add Broth and Corn:**
   - Pour in chicken or vegetable broth and bring to a boil.
   - Add sweet corn and sliced mushrooms if using. Reduce heat and simmer for 10 minutes.
4. **Return Pork and Season:**
   - Return cooked pork to the pot.
   - Add ground ginger and soy sauce if using. Simmer for an additional 5 minutes to allow flavors to meld.
   - Season with salt and freshly ground black pepper to taste.
5. **Serve:**
   - Garnish with fresh cilantro or parsley before serving.

Enjoy your flavorful and hearty Pork and Sweet Corn Soup!

Spiced Carrot Soup

Ingredients:

- **2 tbsp olive oil**
- **1 large onion**, chopped
- **3 cloves garlic**, minced
- **1 tbsp fresh ginger**, minced

- **1 lb (450 g) carrots**, peeled and sliced
- **1 tsp ground cumin**
- **1 tsp ground coriander**
- **1/2 tsp ground cinnamon**
- **1/4 tsp ground turmeric**
- **1/4 tsp cayenne pepper** (optional, for heat)
- **4 cups vegetable or chicken broth**
- **1 cup coconut milk** (or heavy cream for a richer version)
- **Salt and freshly ground black pepper**, to taste
- **1 tbsp fresh lemon juice** (optional, for brightness)
- **Fresh cilantro**, chopped (for garnish)

Instructions:

1. **Sauté Aromatics:**
   - Heat olive oil in a large pot over medium heat.
   - Add chopped onion and cook until softened, about 5 minutes.
   - Stir in minced garlic and fresh ginger, and cook for an additional minute.
2. **Add Carrots and Spices:**
   - Add sliced carrots to the pot and cook for 5 minutes, stirring occasionally.
   - Stir in ground cumin, coriander, cinnamon, turmeric, and cayenne pepper if using. Cook for another 2 minutes until spices are fragrant.
3. **Add Broth and Simmer:**
   - Pour in vegetable or chicken broth and bring to a boil.
   - Reduce heat and simmer until carrots are very tender, about 20 minutes.
4. **Blend the Soup:**
   - Use an immersion blender to blend the soup until smooth. Alternatively, carefully transfer soup in batches to a blender, blend until smooth, and return to the pot.
5. **Add Coconut Milk and Season:**
   - Stir in coconut milk and heat through.
   - Season with salt and freshly ground black pepper to taste.
   - Add fresh lemon juice if desired for extra brightness.
6. **Serve:**
   - Ladle soup into bowls and garnish with fresh cilantro.

Enjoy your spicy and comforting Carrot Soup!

Pea and Ham Soup

Ingredients:

- 1 tbsp olive oil
- 1 onion, chopped
- 2 garlic cloves, minced
- 2 carrots, diced
- 2 celery stalks, diced
- 1 cup split peas, rinsed

- 4 cups chicken or vegetable broth
- 1 ham hock or 1 cup diced ham
- 1 bay leaf
- Salt and pepper to taste
- Optional: 1 tsp thyme or parsley for added flavor

Instructions:

1. Heat olive oil in a large pot over medium heat. Add onion and garlic, sauté until soft.
2. Add carrots and celery, cook for 5 minutes.
3. Stir in split peas, broth, ham hock, and bay leaf. Bring to a boil.
4. Reduce heat, cover, and simmer for 1-1.5 hours, until peas are tender and soup is thickened.
5. Remove ham hock, shred meat, and return to soup. Season with salt, pepper, and optional herbs.
6. Serve hot. Enjoy!

Chicken and Dumplings Soup

Ingredients:

- 1 tbsp olive oil
- 1 onion, chopped
- 2 garlic cloves, minced
- 2 carrots, sliced
- 2 celery stalks, sliced
- 1 lb chicken breasts or thighs, diced

- 6 cups chicken broth
- 1 cup frozen peas
- 1 cup heavy cream
- 1 tsp dried thyme
- 1 bay leaf
- Salt and pepper to taste

For Dumplings:

- 1 cup all-purpose flour
- 1 ½ tsp baking powder
- ¼ tsp salt
- ¼ cup cold butter
- ¾ cup milk

Instructions:

1. Heat olive oil in a large pot. Sauté onion and garlic until soft.
2. Add carrots, celery, and chicken; cook until chicken is browned.
3. Pour in chicken broth, peas, thyme, and bay leaf. Bring to a boil.
4. Reduce heat and simmer for 20 minutes.
5. For dumplings: In a bowl, mix flour, baking powder, and salt. Cut in butter until crumbly. Stir in milk to form a dough.
6. Drop spoonfuls of dough into simmering soup. Cover and cook for 15 minutes, or until dumplings are cooked through.
7. Stir in heavy cream, season with salt and pepper, and serve.

Sweet Potato and Black Bean Soup

Ingredients:

- 1 tbsp olive oil
- 1 onion, chopped
- 2 garlic cloves, minced
- 1 bell pepper (any color), diced
- 2 medium sweet potatoes, peeled and diced
- 1 can (15 oz) black beans, drained and rinsed

- 1 can (14.5 oz) diced tomatoes
- 4 cups vegetable broth
- 1 tsp ground cumin
- 1 tsp smoked paprika
- ½ tsp chili powder (adjust to taste)
- Salt and pepper to taste
- Optional: 1 cup corn kernels (fresh, frozen, or canned)
- Optional: 1 lime, juiced (for serving)
- Optional garnishes: chopped cilantro, avocado, sour cream

Instructions:

1. Heat olive oil in a large pot over medium heat. Add onion and garlic, and cook until softened.
2. Add bell pepper, sweet potatoes, cumin, smoked paprika, chili powder, salt, and pepper. Cook for another 5 minutes, stirring occasionally.
3. Stir in black beans, diced tomatoes, and vegetable broth. Bring to a boil.
4. Reduce heat and simmer for 20-25 minutes, or until sweet potatoes are tender.
5. (Optional) If using corn, stir it in during the last 5 minutes of cooking.
6. Taste and adjust seasoning if needed. If you like, add lime juice for a fresh touch.
7. Serve hot, garnished with cilantro, avocado, and a dollop of sour cream if desired.

Egg Drop Soup

Ingredients:

- 4 cups chicken or vegetable broth
- 1 tbsp cornstarch mixed with 2 tbsp water (for thickening)
- 2 large eggs, lightly beaten
- 1 tbsp soy sauce
- 1 tsp sesame oil
- 1/2 tsp grated ginger (optional)

- Salt and white pepper to taste
- Chopped green onions for garnish

Instructions:

1. Bring broth to a boil in a pot. Add soy sauce, sesame oil, and ginger if using.
2. Stir in the cornstarch mixture and cook until the soup slightly thickens.
3. Reduce heat to a simmer. Slowly pour in the beaten eggs while stirring gently to form egg ribbons.
4. Season with salt and white pepper. Garnish with chopped green onions before serving.

Rustic Vegetable Soup

Ingredients:

- 2 tbsp olive oil
- 1 onion, chopped
- 3 garlic cloves, minced
- 2 carrots, diced
- 2 celery stalks, diced
- 1 bell pepper, diced

- 2 potatoes, peeled and diced
- 1 zucchini, diced
- 1 cup green beans, chopped
- 1 can (14.5 oz) diced tomatoes
- 4 cups vegetable broth
- 1 tsp dried basil
- 1 tsp dried thyme
- Salt and pepper to taste

Instructions:

1. Heat olive oil in a large pot over medium heat. Add onion and garlic, cook until softened.
2. Add carrots, celery, and bell pepper; cook for 5 minutes.
3. Stir in potatoes, zucchini, green beans, tomatoes, broth, basil, and thyme. Bring to a boil.
4. Reduce heat and simmer for 20-30 minutes, until vegetables are tender.
5. Season with salt and pepper, and serve hot.

Greek Lemon Chicken Soup (Avgolemono)

Ingredients:

- 1 tbsp olive oil
- 1 onion, chopped
- 2 garlic cloves, minced
- 1 cup carrots, sliced
- 1 cup celery, sliced
- 1 lb boneless, skinless chicken breasts or thighs

- 6 cups chicken broth
- 1 cup orzo or rice
- 3 large eggs
- 1/2 cup fresh lemon juice (about 2 lemons)
- Salt and pepper to taste
- Optional: chopped fresh parsley for garnish

Instructions:

1. Heat olive oil in a large pot over medium heat. Add onion and garlic, and cook until softened.
2. Add carrots, celery, and chicken. Cook for a few minutes until chicken is no longer pink.
3. Pour in chicken broth and bring to a boil. Reduce heat and simmer for 15-20 minutes, or until chicken is cooked through.
4. Remove chicken from the pot and shred or dice it. Return the chicken to the pot.
5. Stir in orzo or rice and cook according to package instructions until tender.
6. In a separate bowl, whisk together eggs and lemon juice.
7. Gradually add a few ladlefuls of hot soup to the egg-lemon mixture, whisking constantly to temper the eggs.
8. Slowly stir the tempered egg mixture back into the soup, stirring gently to combine. Heat the soup gently but do not let it boil.
9. Season with salt and pepper. Garnish with parsley if desired.

Enjoy your Avgolemono!

Roasted Tomato and Garlic Soup

Ingredients:

- 2 lbs ripe tomatoes (about 8-10 medium), quartered
- 1 head garlic, top sliced off
- 2 tbsp olive oil
- 1 onion, chopped
- 4 cups vegetable or chicken broth
- 1 tsp dried basil

- 1 tsp dried thyme
- Salt and pepper to taste
- 1 tbsp balsamic vinegar (optional)
- Fresh basil or parsley for garnish (optional)
- 1/2 cup heavy cream or coconut milk (optional for creaminess)

Instructions:

1. Preheat your oven to 400°F (200°C).
2. Place the quartered tomatoes and the whole head of garlic on a baking sheet. Drizzle with olive oil and season with salt and pepper.
3. Roast in the oven for 30-35 minutes, or until tomatoes are soft and slightly caramelized, and the garlic is tender.
4. Remove from the oven and let cool slightly. Squeeze the roasted garlic cloves out of their skins.
5. Heat a large pot over medium heat. Add a bit of olive oil and sauté the chopped onion until translucent.
6. Add the roasted tomatoes and garlic to the pot, along with the vegetable or chicken broth, basil, and thyme. Bring to a simmer and cook for 10 minutes to blend the flavors.
7. Use an immersion blender to puree the soup until smooth. Alternatively, transfer the soup in batches to a blender and blend until smooth, then return to the pot.
8. Stir in balsamic vinegar if using, and adjust seasoning with salt and pepper. For a creamy soup, add heavy cream or coconut milk and heat through.
9. Serve hot, garnished with fresh basil or parsley if desired.

Enjoy your homemade roasted tomato and garlic soup!

Spicy Sausage and Kale Soup

Ingredients:

- 1 tbsp olive oil
- 1 lb spicy Italian sausage (bulk, not in casings), crumbled
- 1 onion, chopped
- 3 garlic cloves, minced
- 2 carrots, sliced
- 2 celery stalks, sliced

- 1 bell pepper (any color), diced
- 1 can (14.5 oz) diced tomatoes
- 4 cups chicken or vegetable broth
- 1 tsp dried oregano
- 1 tsp smoked paprika
- 1/2 tsp red pepper flakes (adjust to taste)
- 1 bunch kale, stems removed and leaves torn
- 1 cup cooked pasta or rice (optional)
- Salt and pepper to taste

Instructions:

1. Heat olive oil in a large pot over medium heat. Add crumbled sausage and cook until browned. Remove sausage from the pot and set aside.
2. In the same pot, add onion, garlic, carrots, celery, and bell pepper. Cook until vegetables are tender.
3. Stir in diced tomatoes, broth, oregano, smoked paprika, and red pepper flakes. Bring to a boil.
4. Reduce heat and simmer for 15 minutes.
5. Return the sausage to the pot and add kale. Cook for another 5-7 minutes, until kale is wilted and tender.
6. If using pasta or rice, stir it in and cook until heated through.
7. Season with salt and pepper to taste. Serve hot. Enjoy!

Simple Pho

Ingredients:

- 1 lb beef sirloin or brisket, thinly sliced
- 1 onion, halved
- 1 piece ginger (2 inches), sliced
- 4 cups beef broth
- 2 cups water
- 2-3 star anise

- 1 cinnamon stick
- 3-4 cloves
- 2 tbsp fish sauce
- 1 tbsp soy sauce
- 200g rice noodles (banh pho), cooked according to package instructions
- Fresh herbs: cilantro, basil, and mint
- Bean sprouts
- Lime wedges
- Sliced jalapeños or chilies (optional)
- Thinly sliced onions (for garnish)

Instructions:

1. Char onion and ginger by placing them under a broiler or over an open flame until slightly blackened.
2. In a large pot, combine beef broth, water, charred onion, ginger, star anise, cinnamon stick, and cloves. Bring to a boil, then reduce heat and simmer for 15-20 minutes.
3. Strain the broth to remove solids, then return it to the pot. Stir in fish sauce and soy sauce.
4. Add thinly sliced beef to the broth and cook until just tender, about 1-2 minutes.
5. Divide cooked rice noodles among bowls. Ladle hot broth and beef over the noodles.
6. Garnish with fresh herbs, bean sprouts, lime wedges, sliced jalapeños, and onions. Serve hot.

Italian Sausage Soup with Kale

Ingredients:

- 1 tbsp olive oil
- 1 lb Italian sausage (bulk, not in casings), crumbled
- 1 onion, chopped
- 3 garlic cloves, minced
- 2 carrots, sliced
- 2 celery stalks, sliced

- 1 bell pepper, diced
- 1 can (14.5 oz) diced tomatoes
- 4 cups chicken or vegetable broth
- 1 tsp dried oregano
- 1 tsp dried basil
- 1/2 tsp red pepper flakes (optional, adjust to taste)
- 1 bunch kale, stems removed and leaves torn
- 1 cup cooked pasta or beans (optional)
- Salt and pepper to taste
- Optional: grated Parmesan cheese for serving

Instructions:

1. Heat olive oil in a large pot over medium heat. Add crumbled sausage and cook until browned. Remove sausage from the pot and set aside.
2. In the same pot, add onion, garlic, carrots, celery, and bell pepper. Cook until vegetables are tender, about 5-7 minutes.
3. Stir in diced tomatoes, broth, oregano, basil, and red pepper flakes. Bring to a boil.
4. Reduce heat and simmer for 10-15 minutes.
5. Return the sausage to the pot and add kale. Cook until kale is wilted and tender, about 5 minutes.
6. If using cooked pasta or beans, stir them in and cook until heated through.
7. Season with salt and pepper to taste. Serve hot, optionally garnished with grated Parmesan cheese.

Enjoy your Italian Sausage Soup with Kale!

Cheesy Cauliflower Soup

Ingredients:

- 1 tbsp olive oil
- 1 onion, chopped
- 3 garlic cloves, minced
- 1 large head cauliflower, chopped
- 4 cups vegetable or chicken broth
- 1 cup milk

- 1 cup shredded cheddar cheese
- 1/2 tsp dried thyme
- Salt and pepper to taste
- Optional: 1/4 cup grated Parmesan cheese
- Optional: chopped chives for garnish

Instructions:

1. Heat olive oil in a large pot over medium heat. Add onion and garlic, cooking until softened.
2. Add cauliflower and broth. Bring to a boil, then reduce heat and simmer until cauliflower is tender, about 15-20 minutes.
3. Use an immersion blender to puree the soup until smooth. Alternatively, transfer in batches to a blender.
4. Stir in milk and cheddar cheese until melted and smooth. Add thyme, salt, and pepper.
5. For extra richness, stir in Parmesan cheese if using.
6. Garnish with chopped chives if desired. Serve hot. Enjoy!

Creamy Shrimp and Corn Soup

Ingredients:

- 1 tbsp olive oil
- 1 lb shrimp, peeled and deveined
- 1 onion, chopped
- 3 garlic cloves, minced
- 2 cups fresh or frozen corn kernels
- 1 large potato, peeled and diced

- 4 cups chicken or vegetable broth
- 1 cup heavy cream
- 1/2 cup milk
- 1 tsp smoked paprika
- 1/2 tsp dried thyme
- Salt and pepper to taste
- 2 tbsp fresh parsley or chives, chopped (for garnish)

Instructions:

1. Heat olive oil in a large pot over medium heat. Add onion and garlic, and cook until softened.
2. Add shrimp to the pot and cook until pink and opaque, about 2-3 minutes per side. Remove shrimp and set aside.
3. Add corn kernels and diced potato to the pot. Stir for a couple of minutes.
4. Pour in the broth and bring to a boil. Reduce heat and simmer until potatoes are tender, about 10-15 minutes.
5. Use an immersion blender to puree the soup until smooth. Alternatively, blend in batches using a regular blender.
6. Stir in the heavy cream, milk, smoked paprika, and thyme. Heat through but do not boil.
7. Return the cooked shrimp to the pot. Adjust seasoning with salt and pepper.
8. Garnish with fresh parsley or chives before serving. Enjoy your creamy shrimp and corn soup!

Beef Stroganoff Soup

Ingredients:

- 2 tbsp olive oil
- 1 lb beef stew meat or sirloin, cut into bite-sized pieces
- 1 onion, chopped
- 3 garlic cloves, minced
- 2 cups mushrooms, sliced
- 2 cups beef broth

- 1 cup water
- 1 cup sour cream
- 1 cup heavy cream
- 2 tbsp all-purpose flour
- 1 tsp dried thyme
- 1 tsp paprika
- Salt and pepper to taste
- 2 tbsp Worcestershire sauce
- 1 cup egg noodles or pasta of choice (optional)
- Fresh parsley, chopped (for garnish)

Instructions:

1. Heat olive oil in a large pot over medium-high heat. Add beef pieces and cook until browned on all sides. Remove the beef and set aside.
2. In the same pot, add onion, garlic, and mushrooms. Cook until the mushrooms are tender and the onions are translucent.
3. Stir in flour and cook for 1-2 minutes to form a roux.
4. Add beef broth, water, thyme, paprika, and Worcestershire sauce. Stir to combine and bring to a boil.
5. Reduce heat and simmer for about 10-15 minutes, or until beef is tender and cooked through.
6. If using, add egg noodles or pasta and cook according to package instructions.
7. Stir in sour cream and heavy cream, and heat through, but do not boil. Adjust seasoning with salt and pepper.
8. Garnish with fresh parsley before serving.

Enjoy your comforting Beef Stroganoff Soup!

Cabbage Roll Soup

Ingredients:

- 1 tbsp olive oil
- 1 lb ground beef or pork (or a mix)
- 1 onion, chopped
- 3 garlic cloves, minced
- 1 large carrot, diced
- 2 celery stalks, diced

- 1/2 cup uncooked rice (white or brown)
- 1 can (14.5 oz) diced tomatoes
- 4 cups beef or vegetable broth
- 1 small head of cabbage, chopped (about 4 cups)
- 1 tsp dried oregano
- 1 tsp dried basil
- 1/2 tsp paprika
- 1/2 tsp caraway seeds (optional)
- Salt and pepper to taste
- 2 tbsp fresh parsley, chopped (for garnish)
- Optional: 1 tbsp lemon juice or vinegar (for added tang)

Instructions:

1. Heat olive oil in a large pot over medium heat. Add ground beef or pork and cook until browned, breaking it up with a spoon. Drain excess fat if necessary.
2. Add onion and garlic to the pot, cooking until softened.
3. Stir in carrots, celery, and rice, cooking for 2-3 minutes.
4. Add diced tomatoes, broth, cabbage, oregano, basil, paprika, and caraway seeds if using. Bring to a boil.
5. Reduce heat and simmer for 25-30 minutes, or until rice is cooked and cabbage is tender.
6. Season with salt and pepper to taste. Stir in lemon juice or vinegar if desired for added flavor.
7. Garnish with fresh parsley before serving.

Enjoy your comforting and flavorful Cabbage Roll Soup!

Sweet and Sour Soup

Ingredients:

- 1 tbsp vegetable oil
- 1 onion, chopped
- 2 garlic cloves, minced
- 1 bell pepper (any color), diced
- 1 cup carrots, sliced
- 1 cup mushrooms, sliced

- 4 cups chicken or vegetable broth
- 1 cup pineapple chunks (fresh or canned), with juice
- 1/4 cup rice vinegar
- 1/4 cup soy sauce
- 2 tbsp brown sugar or honey
- 1 tbsp cornstarch mixed with 2 tbsp water (for thickening)
- 1 cup cooked shredded chicken or tofu (optional)
- Salt and pepper to taste
- Optional: 1/4 tsp red pepper flakes (for heat)
- Optional garnishes: chopped cilantro, sliced green onions

Instructions:

1. Heat vegetable oil in a large pot over medium heat. Add onion and garlic, and cook until softened.
2. Add bell pepper, carrots, and mushrooms. Cook for another 5 minutes until vegetables start to soften.
3. Pour in the broth, pineapple chunks with juice, rice vinegar, soy sauce, and brown sugar or honey. Bring to a boil.
4. Reduce heat and simmer for 10 minutes.
5. Stir in the cornstarch mixture and cook until the soup thickens slightly, about 2 minutes.
6. If using, add cooked shredded chicken or tofu. Heat through.
7. Season with salt, pepper, and red pepper flakes if using.
8. Garnish with chopped cilantro and sliced green onions if desired.

Enjoy your Sweet and Sour Soup!

Poblano Pepper Soup

Ingredients:

- 2 tbsp olive oil
- 1 onion, chopped
- 3 garlic cloves, minced
- 4-5 poblano peppers, roasted, peeled, and diced
- 1 bell pepper (any color), diced
- 2 cups vegetable or chicken broth

- 1 cup heavy cream or coconut milk
- 1 tsp ground cumin
- 1 tsp smoked paprika
- 1/2 tsp dried oregano
- Salt and pepper to taste
- Optional: 1-2 tbsp lime juice (for brightness)
- Optional garnishes: chopped cilantro, avocado, crumbled queso fresco, tortilla chips

Instructions:

1. **Roast Poblano Peppers**: Preheat your oven's broiler. Place the poblano peppers on a baking sheet and roast under the broiler, turning occasionally, until the skins are blackened and blistered. Alternatively, you can roast them over a gas flame. Place the roasted peppers in a bowl, cover with plastic wrap, and let them steam for about 10 minutes. This will make peeling easier. Peel off the skins, remove seeds and stems, and dice the peppers.
2. **Cook Vegetables**: Heat olive oil in a large pot over medium heat. Add the chopped onion and cook until translucent. Add garlic and cook for another minute until fragrant.
3. **Add Peppers and Broth**: Stir in the diced poblano peppers, bell pepper, and cook for a few minutes. Add the vegetable or chicken broth, ground cumin, smoked paprika, and oregano. Bring to a boil, then reduce heat and simmer for about 10 minutes.
4. **Blend Soup**: Use an immersion blender to blend the soup until smooth. Alternatively, carefully transfer the soup in batches to a blender and blend until smooth. Return the soup to the pot.
5. **Add Cream and Adjust Seasoning**: Stir in the heavy cream or coconut milk. Heat through, but do not let it boil. Adjust seasoning with salt, pepper, and lime juice if using.
6. **Serve**: Garnish with chopped cilantro, avocado slices, crumbled queso fresco, or tortilla chips if desired. Serve hot.

Enjoy your creamy and spicy Poblano Pepper Soup!

Goulash Soup

Ingredients:

- 2 tbsp olive oil
- 1 lb beef stew meat or chuck, cut into cubes
- 1 onion, chopped
- 3 garlic cloves, minced
- 2 bell peppers (any color), diced
- 2 cups potatoes, peeled and diced

- 2 carrots, sliced
- 1 can (14.5 oz) diced tomatoes
- 4 cups beef broth
- 2 tbsp paprika (preferably Hungarian)
- 1 tsp caraway seeds (optional)
- 1 tsp dried thyme
- 1 bay leaf
- Salt and pepper to taste
- Optional: 1 cup frozen peas
- Optional: 1-2 tbsp vinegar or lemon juice (for tanginess)
- Fresh parsley for garnish

Instructions:

1. **Brown the Meat**: Heat olive oil in a large pot over medium-high heat. Add beef cubes and brown on all sides. Remove the meat and set aside.
2. **Sauté Vegetables**: In the same pot, add onion and garlic. Cook until softened. Add bell peppers, potatoes, and carrots. Cook for a few minutes.
3. **Add Spices and Broth**: Stir in paprika, caraway seeds, thyme, and bay leaf. Return the beef to the pot. Add diced tomatoes and beef broth. Bring to a boil.
4. **Simmer**: Reduce heat and simmer for 30-40 minutes, or until beef and vegetables are tender.
5. **Finish**: If using, stir in frozen peas and cook for another 5 minutes. Adjust seasoning with salt, pepper, and vinegar or lemon juice if desired.
6. **Serve**: Garnish with fresh parsley and serve hot.

Enjoy your warming Goulash Soup!

Creamy Celery Soup

Ingredients:

- 2 tbsp butter
- 1 onion, chopped
- 3 garlic cloves, minced
- 4 cups celery, chopped (including some leaves if available)
- 2 cups vegetable or chicken broth
- 1 cup milk or cream

- 1 tsp dried thyme
- Salt and pepper to taste
- Optional: 1/4 cup grated Parmesan cheese
- Optional garnishes: chopped fresh parsley, a drizzle of cream, or croutons

Instructions:

1. **Sauté Vegetables**: Melt butter in a large pot over medium heat. Add onion and garlic, cooking until softened.
2. **Cook Celery**: Add chopped celery and cook for about 5 minutes until it starts to soften.
3. **Add Broth and Simmer**: Pour in the broth and add thyme. Bring to a boil, then reduce heat and simmer for 15-20 minutes, until celery is very tender.
4. **Blend Soup**: Use an immersion blender to puree the soup until smooth. Alternatively, blend in batches using a regular blender.
5. **Add Cream**: Stir in the milk or cream, and heat through. For extra richness, you can also add grated Parmesan cheese.
6. **Season and Serve**: Adjust seasoning with salt and pepper. Garnish with fresh parsley, a drizzle of cream, or croutons if desired.

Enjoy your creamy celery soup!

Coconut Curry Soup

Ingredients:

- 1 tbsp coconut oil or olive oil
- 1 onion, chopped
- 3 garlic cloves, minced
- 1 tbsp fresh ginger, grated
- 2-3 tbsp curry powder (adjust to taste)
- 1 tbsp turmeric powder (optional, for color)

- 1 can (14 oz) coconut milk
- 4 cups vegetable or chicken broth
- 2 cups vegetables of choice (e.g., bell peppers, carrots, sweet potatoes, or cauliflower)
- 1-2 tbsp soy sauce or tamari (for seasoning)
- Salt and pepper to taste
- Optional: 1 tbsp lime juice (for brightness)
- Optional garnishes: chopped cilantro, sliced green onions, or a dollop of yogurt

Instructions:

1. **Sauté Aromatics**: Heat coconut oil in a large pot over medium heat. Add onion, garlic, and ginger. Cook until softened and fragrant.
2. **Add Spices**: Stir in curry powder and turmeric, cooking for 1-2 minutes to bloom the spices.
3. **Add Liquids and Vegetables**: Pour in coconut milk and broth. Add vegetables and bring to a boil. Reduce heat and simmer until vegetables are tender, about 10-15 minutes.
4. **Season and Finish**: Stir in soy sauce or tamari. Adjust seasoning with salt, pepper, and lime juice if using.
5. **Serve**: Garnish with chopped cilantro, sliced green onions, or a dollop of yogurt if desired. Serve hot.

Enjoy your rich and aromatic Coconut Curry Soup!

Buffalo Chicken Soup

Ingredients:

- 1 tbsp olive oil
- 1 lb cooked chicken (shredded or diced)
- 1 onion, chopped
- 3 garlic cloves, minced
- 2 carrots, diced
- 2 celery stalks, diced
- 4 cups chicken broth

- 1 cup milk or cream
- 1/2 cup Buffalo sauce (adjust to taste)
- 1 tsp dried thyme
- 1/2 tsp paprika
- Salt and pepper to taste
- Optional: 1 cup shredded cheddar cheese
- Optional garnishes: chopped green onions, crumbled blue cheese, or celery sticks

Instructions:

1. **Sauté Vegetables**: Heat olive oil in a large pot over medium heat. Add onion, garlic, carrots, and celery. Cook until vegetables are softened.
2. **Add Broth and Chicken**: Stir in chicken broth and add the cooked chicken. Bring to a boil, then reduce heat and simmer for 10 minutes.
3. **Add Flavorings**: Stir in milk or cream, Buffalo sauce, thyme, and paprika. Heat through, but do not boil.
4. **Optional Cheese**: If using, stir in shredded cheddar cheese until melted and smooth.
5. **Season and Serve**: Adjust seasoning with salt and pepper. Garnish with chopped green onions, crumbled blue cheese, or celery sticks if desired.

Enjoy your tangy and comforting Buffalo Chicken Soup!

Lentil and Spinach Soup

Ingredients:

- 1 tbsp olive oil
- 1 onion, chopped
- 3 garlic cloves, minced
- 2 carrots, diced
- 2 celery stalks, diced
- 1 cup dried green or brown lentils, rinsed
- 1 can (14.5 oz) diced tomatoes

- 4 cups vegetable or chicken broth
- 1 tsp ground cumin
- 1 tsp smoked paprika
- 1/2 tsp dried thyme
- 2 cups fresh spinach, chopped
- Salt and pepper to taste
- Optional: 1-2 tbsp lemon juice (for brightness)

Instructions:

1. **Sauté Vegetables**: Heat olive oil in a large pot over medium heat. Add onion, garlic, carrots, and celery. Cook until softened.
2. **Add Lentils and Spices**: Stir in lentils, cumin, smoked paprika, and thyme. Cook for 1-2 minutes.
3. **Add Liquids**: Pour in diced tomatoes and broth. Bring to a boil, then reduce heat and simmer for 25-30 minutes, or until lentils are tender.
4. **Add Spinach**: Stir in chopped spinach and cook for another 5 minutes until wilted.
5. **Season and Finish**: Adjust seasoning with salt, pepper, and lemon juice if using.
6. **Serve**: Serve hot, and enjoy!

This soup is hearty and packed with nutrients.

Wild Mushroom Soup

Ingredients:

- 2 tbsp olive oil or unsalted butter
- 1 onion, finely chopped
- 3 garlic cloves, minced
- 1 lb mixed wild mushrooms (e.g., shiitake, cremini, porcini, chanterelles), cleaned and sliced
- 1 cup dried porcini mushrooms (optional, for extra depth of flavor)
- 4 cups vegetable or chicken broth
- 1 cup dry white wine (or additional broth)
- 1 cup heavy cream or coconut milk
- 1 tsp fresh thyme leaves or 1/2 tsp dried thyme
- 1 bay leaf
- Salt and pepper to taste
- Optional: 1 tbsp soy sauce (for umami)
- Optional: 2 tbsp all-purpose flour (for thickening)
- Optional garnishes: chopped fresh parsley, a drizzle of truffle oil, or sautéed mushroom slices

Instructions:

1. **Prepare Dried Mushrooms** (if using): If using dried porcini mushrooms, soak them in warm water for about 30 minutes. Drain and reserve the soaking liquid, then chop the mushrooms.
2. **Sauté Aromatics**: Heat olive oil or butter in a large pot over medium heat. Add onion and cook until translucent. Add garlic and cook for another minute.
3. **Cook Mushrooms**: Add fresh and chopped dried mushrooms to the pot. Cook until mushrooms are browned and their moisture has evaporated, about 10 minutes.
4. **Add Liquids and Simmer**: Pour in the white wine (or extra broth), scraping up any browned bits from the bottom of the pot. Add the broth, thyme, and bay leaf. Bring to a boil, then reduce heat and simmer for 15-20 minutes.
5. **Blend Soup**: Remove the bay leaf. Use an immersion blender to puree the soup until smooth. Alternatively, blend in batches using a regular blender.
6. **Add Cream and Season**: Stir in the heavy cream or coconut milk. If you prefer a thicker soup, you can whisk in 2 tbsp of flour at this point. Adjust seasoning with salt, pepper, and soy sauce if using.
7. **Serve**: Garnish with chopped fresh parsley, a drizzle of truffle oil, or additional sautéed mushrooms if desired.

Enjoy your luxurious and savory Wild Mushroom Soup!

Chicken and Orzo Soup

Ingredients:

- 2 tbsp olive oil
- 1 lb boneless, skinless chicken breasts or thighs, diced
- 1 onion, chopped
- 3 garlic cloves, minced
- 2 carrots, diced
- 2 celery stalks, diced
- 1 bell pepper, diced (optional)
- 4 cups chicken broth
- 1 cup water (or more broth)
- 1 cup orzo pasta
- 1 cup frozen peas or corn
- 1 tsp dried thyme
- 1 tsp dried oregano
- 1 bay leaf
- Salt and pepper to taste
- 2 cups fresh spinach or kale, chopped
- Optional: 1-2 tbsp lemon juice (for brightness)
- Optional: Grated Parmesan cheese for serving

Instructions:

1. **Sauté Chicken**: Heat olive oil in a large pot over medium heat. Add diced chicken and cook until browned and cooked through. Remove chicken from the pot and set aside.
2. **Sauté Vegetables**: In the same pot, add onion, garlic, carrots, celery, and bell pepper if using. Cook until vegetables are softened.
3. **Add Broth and Simmer**: Pour in the chicken broth and water. Stir in thyme, oregano, and bay leaf. Bring to a boil.
4. **Cook Orzo**: Add the orzo pasta and cook according to package instructions, usually about 8-10 minutes, until tender.
5. **Add Chicken and Peas**: Return the cooked chicken to the pot and add frozen peas or corn. Cook for an additional 5 minutes.
6. **Finish with Greens**: Stir in chopped spinach or kale until wilted. Adjust seasoning with salt, pepper, and lemon juice if using.
7. **Serve**: Serve hot, optionally topped with grated Parmesan cheese.

Enjoy your hearty and satisfying Chicken and Orzo Soup!

Spicy Tomato and Chickpea Soup

Ingredients:

- 2 tbsp olive oil
- 1 onion, chopped
- 3 garlic cloves, minced
- 1-2 tbsp fresh ginger, minced
- 1-2 tbsp tomato paste
- 1 can (14.5 oz) diced tomatoes
- 1 can (14 oz) chickpeas, drained and rinsed
- 4 cups vegetable or chicken broth
- 1 tsp ground cumin
- 1 tsp smoked paprika
- 1/2 tsp ground coriander
- 1/2 tsp red pepper flakes (adjust to taste)
- 1/2 tsp cayenne pepper (optional, for extra heat)
- 1 tsp dried oregano
- Salt and pepper to taste
- 1 tbsp lemon juice (for brightness)
- Optional: Fresh cilantro or parsley for garnish

Instructions:

1. **Sauté Aromatics**: Heat olive oil in a large pot over medium heat. Add onion and cook until translucent. Add garlic and ginger, and cook for another minute.
2. **Add Spices and Tomato Paste**: Stir in the tomato paste and cook for 2 minutes. Add ground cumin, smoked paprika, coriander, red pepper flakes, and cayenne pepper if using. Cook for another minute to toast the spices.
3. **Add Tomatoes and Broth**: Stir in the diced tomatoes, chickpeas, and broth. Bring to a boil.
4. **Simmer**: Reduce heat and let the soup simmer for 15-20 minutes to blend the flavors.
5. **Adjust Seasoning**: Taste and adjust seasoning with salt, pepper, and lemon juice.
6. **Serve**: Garnish with fresh cilantro or parsley if desired. Serve hot.

Enjoy your spicy and satisfying Tomato and Chickpea Soup!

Smoky Ham and Bean Soup

Ingredients:

- 2 tbsp olive oil
- 1 onion, chopped
- 3 garlic cloves, minced
- 2 carrots, diced
- 2 celery stalks, diced
- 1 smoked ham hock or 1-2 cups diced smoked ham
- 1 cup dried navy beans or great northern beans, soaked overnight and drained (or 2 cans, rinsed)
- 1 can (14.5 oz) diced tomatoes
- 4 cups chicken or vegetable broth
- 1 tsp smoked paprika
- 1/2 tsp ground cumin
- 1/2 tsp dried thyme
- 1 bay leaf
- Salt and pepper to taste
- Optional: 1 cup chopped kale or spinach
- Optional: 1 tbsp apple cider vinegar (for a touch of acidity)

Instructions:

1. **Sauté Vegetables**: Heat olive oil in a large pot over medium heat. Add onion, garlic, carrots, and celery. Cook until vegetables are softened, about 5-7 minutes.
2. **Add Ham and Beans**: Add the smoked ham hock or diced ham to the pot, along with the soaked and drained beans. Stir in the diced tomatoes.
3. **Add Broth and Spices**: Pour in the chicken or vegetable broth. Add smoked paprika, cumin, thyme, and bay leaf. Bring to a boil.
4. **Simmer**: Reduce heat and let the soup simmer for 1 to 1.5 hours if using dried beans, or 30 minutes if using canned beans, until the beans are tender and the flavors are well combined. If using a ham hock, remove it once the soup is done, shred the meat, and return it to the soup.
5. **Finish**: If using, stir in chopped kale or spinach and cook for another 5 minutes until wilted. Adjust seasoning with salt and pepper. Add apple cider vinegar if desired for extra brightness.
6. **Serve**: Serve hot and enjoy!

This Smoky Ham and Bean Soup is perfect for a comforting meal. Enjoy!

Savory Beef and Ale Soup

Ingredients:

- 2 tbsp olive oil
- 1.5 lbs beef stew meat, cut into cubes
- 1 onion, chopped
- 3 garlic cloves, minced
- 2 carrots, diced
- 2 celery stalks, diced
- 1 cup mushrooms, sliced (optional)
- 1 cup ale or stout (such as Guinness)
- 4 cups beef broth
- 1 cup diced tomatoes (with juice)
- 1 tbsp Worcestershire sauce
- 1 tsp dried thyme
- 1 tsp dried rosemary
- 1 bay leaf
- Salt and pepper to taste
- 1 cup frozen peas or corn (optional)
- 2 tbsp all-purpose flour (for thickening, optional)

Instructions:

1. **Brown the Beef**: Heat olive oil in a large pot over medium-high heat. Add beef cubes and brown on all sides. Remove the beef and set aside.
2. **Sauté Vegetables**: In the same pot, add onion, garlic, carrots, celery, and mushrooms if using. Cook until vegetables are softened.
3. **Add Ale and Broth**: Pour in the ale, scraping up any browned bits from the bottom of the pot. Stir in beef broth, diced tomatoes, Worcestershire sauce, thyme, rosemary, and bay leaf. Return the beef to the pot.
4. **Simmer**: Bring the soup to a boil, then reduce heat and simmer for 1 to 1.5 hours, until beef is tender.
5. **Thicken Soup (Optional)**: If you prefer a thicker soup, mix flour with a little water to make a slurry and stir it into the soup. Simmer for an additional 5-10 minutes until thickened.
6. **Add Peas or Corn**: If using, stir in frozen peas or corn and cook for another 5 minutes.
7. **Season and Serve**: Adjust seasoning with salt and pepper. Remove the bay leaf before serving.

Enjoy your hearty and flavorful Savory Beef and Ale Soup!

www.ingramcontent.com/pod-product-compliance
Lightning Source LLC
LaVergne TN
LVHW081318060526
838201LV00055B/2340